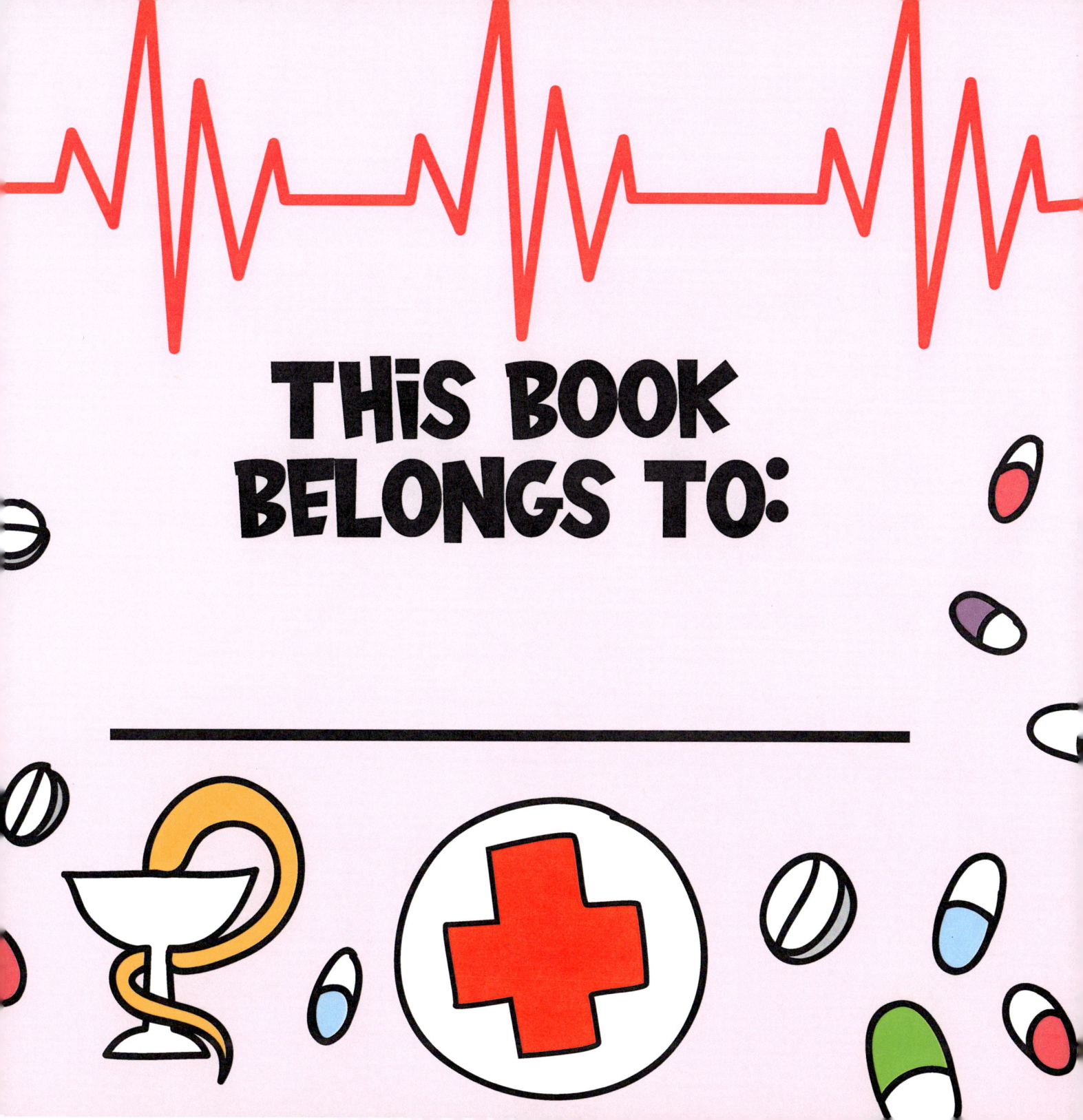

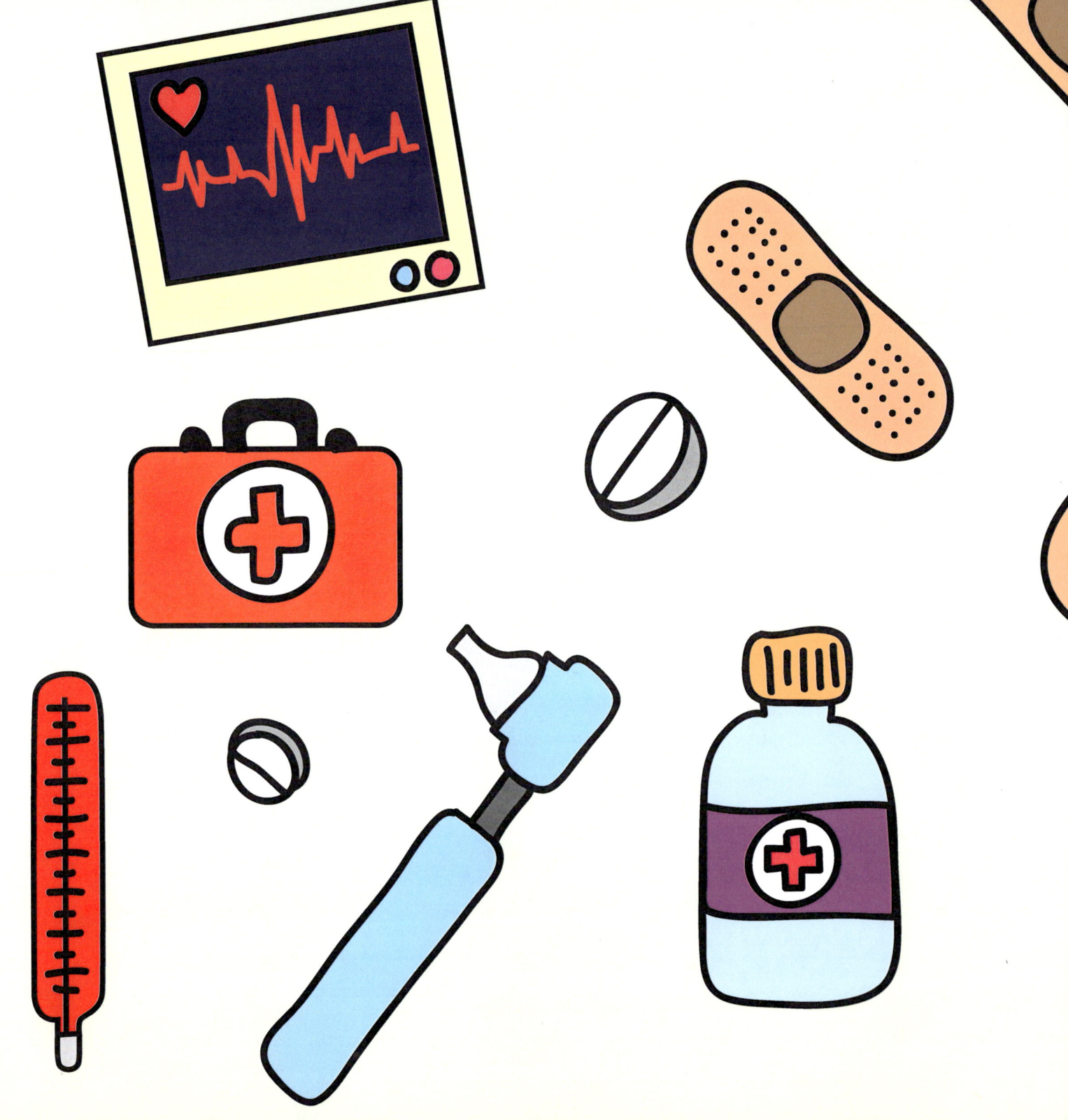

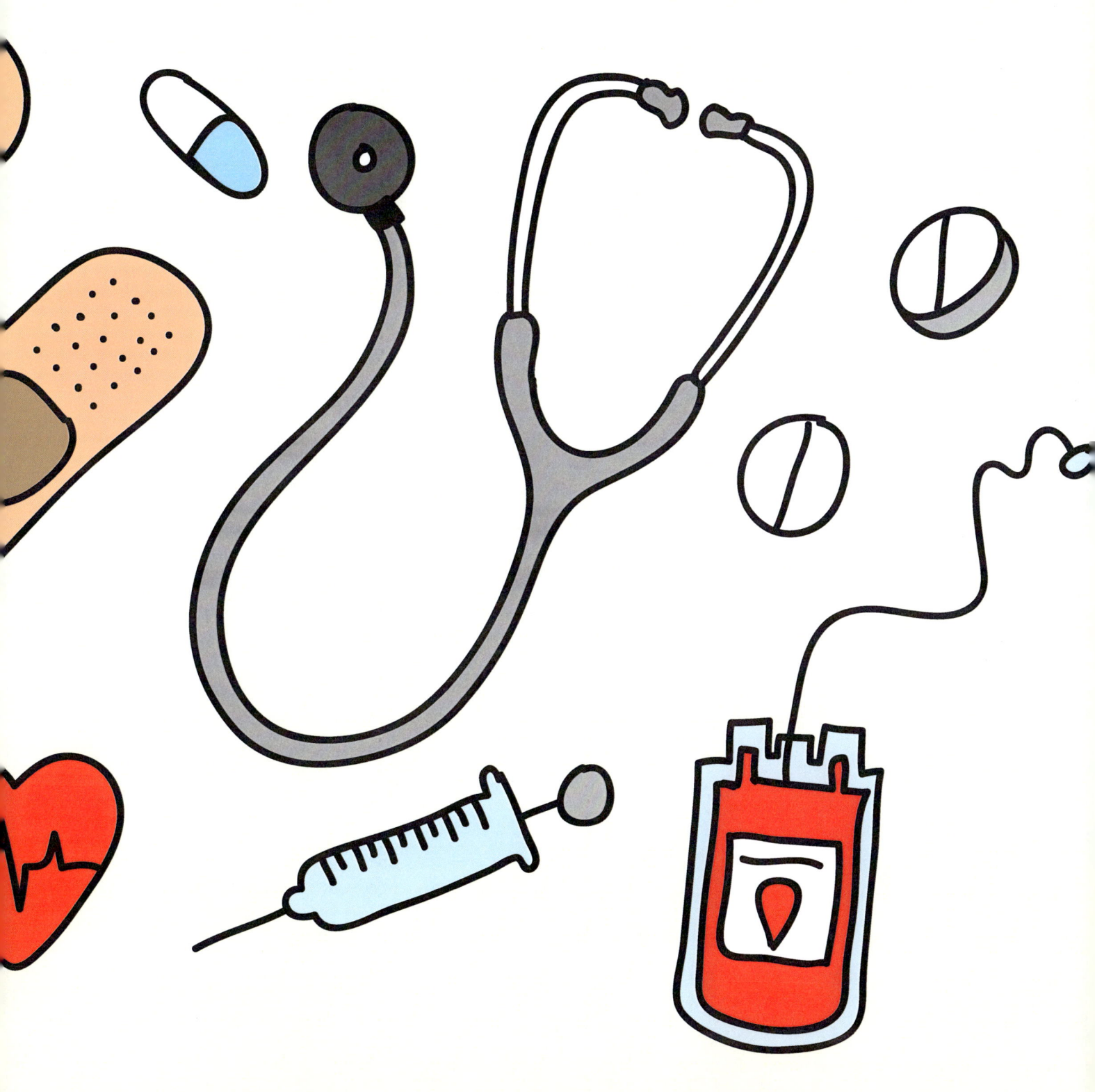

This book is dedicated to my children - Mikey, Kobe, and Jojo.

Copyright © 2024 Grow Grit Press LLC. All rights reserved. No part of this book may be reproduced in any form without permission in writing from the publisher. Please send bulk order requests to info@ninjalifehacks.tv

Paperback ISBN: 978-1-63731-942-0
Hardcover ISBN: 978-1-63731-944-4
eBook ISBN: 978-1-63731-943-7

Printed and bound in the USA.
NinjaLifeHacks.tv

Ninja Life Hacks®
by Mary Nhin

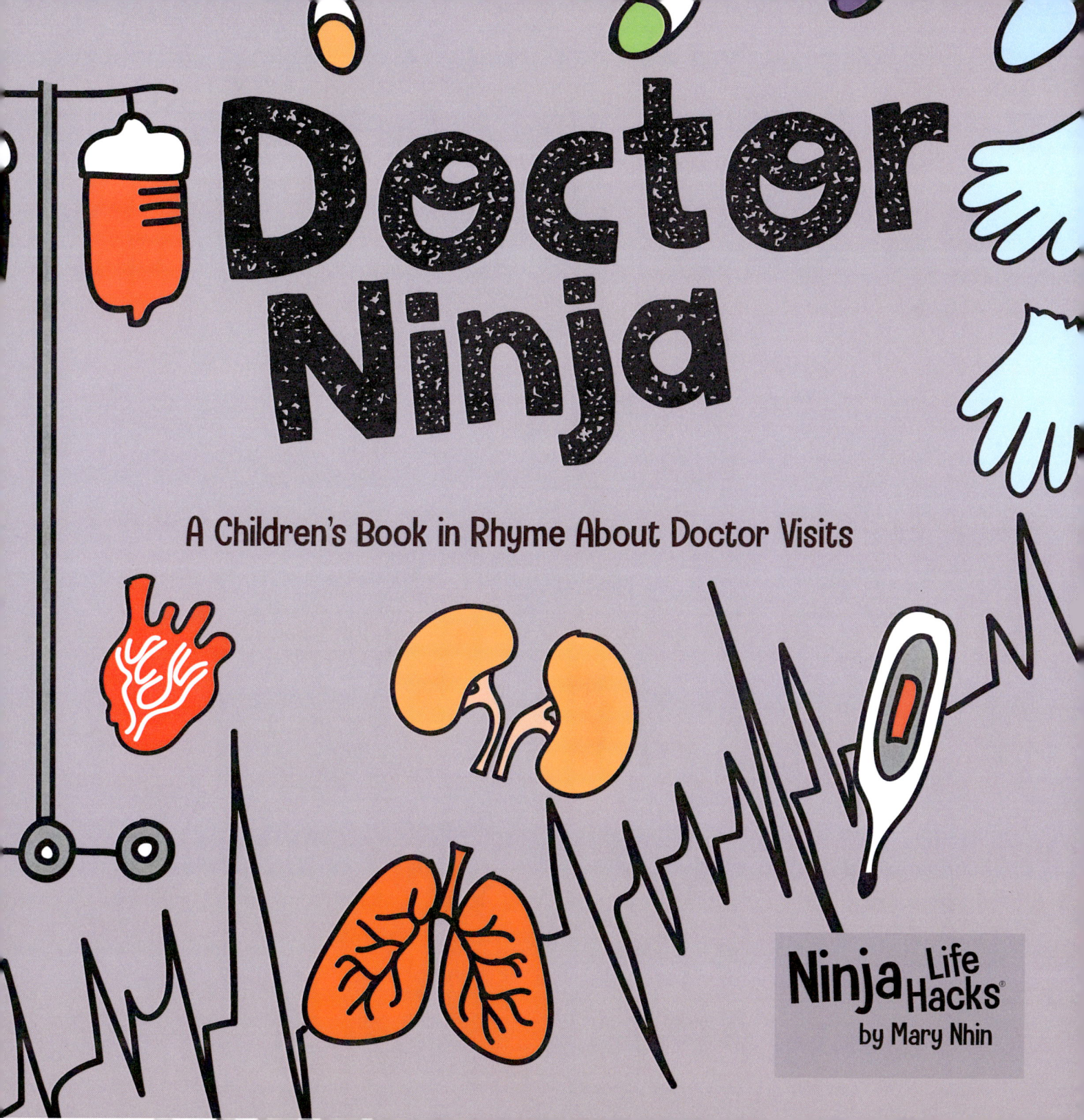

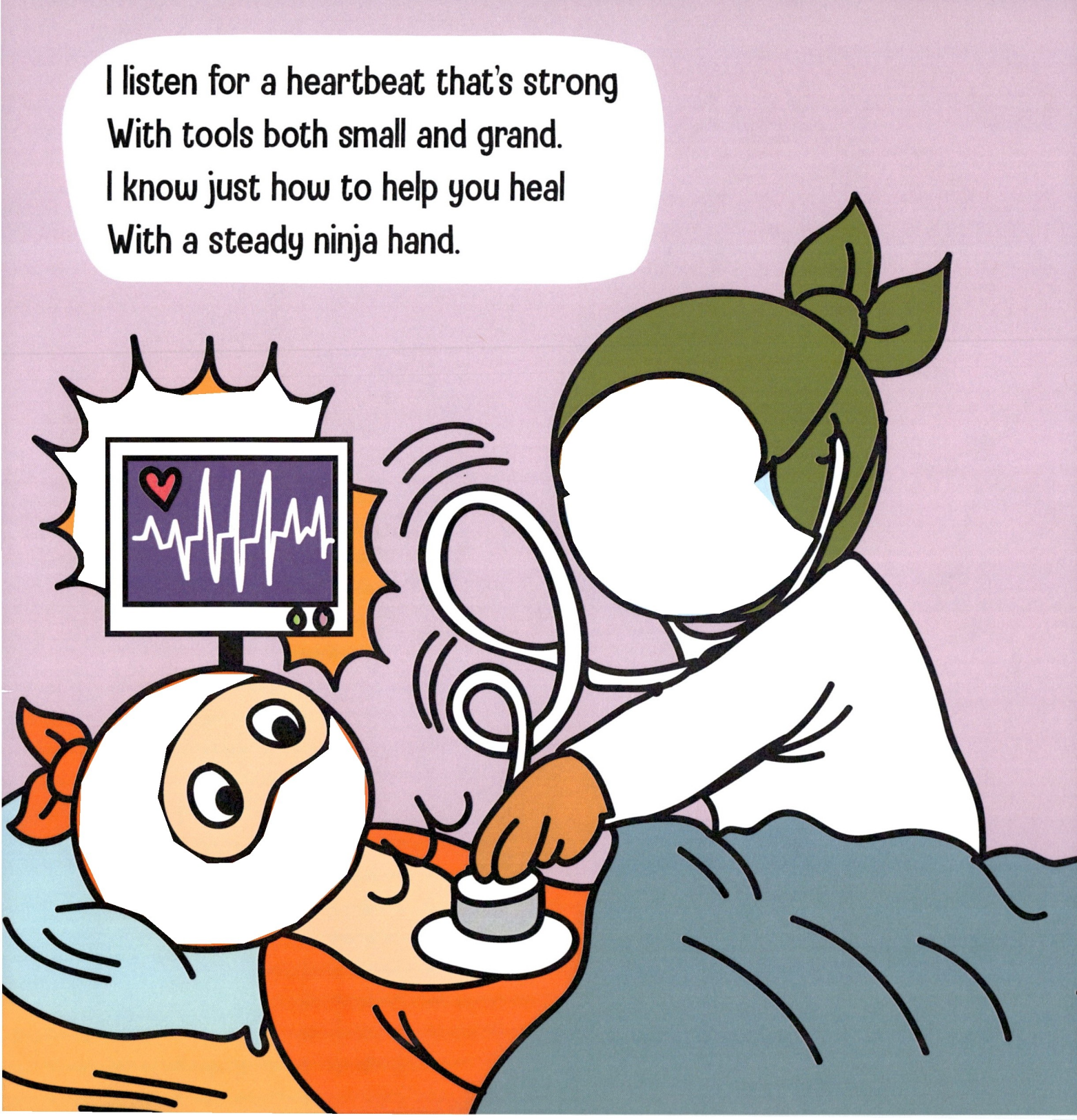

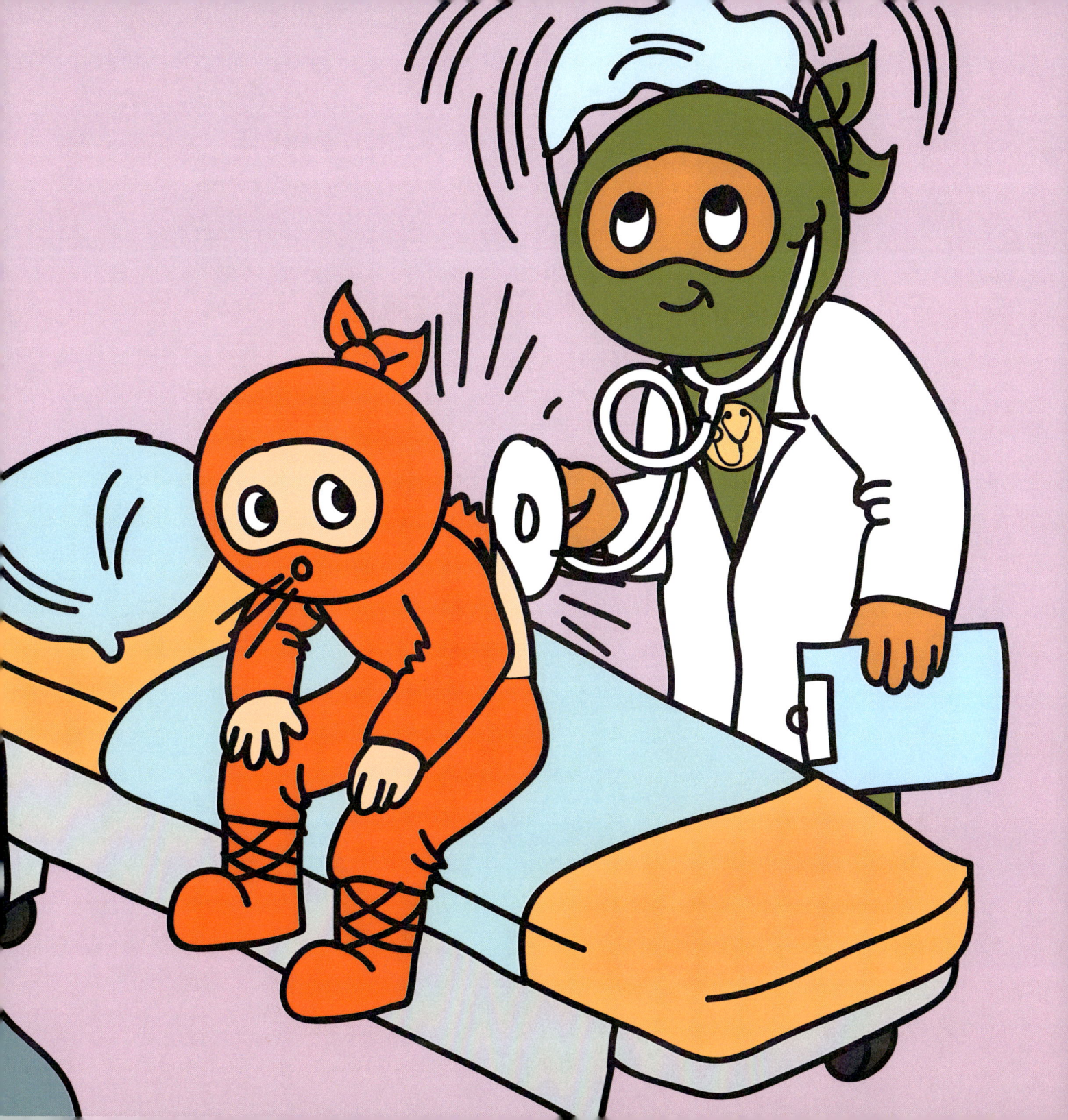

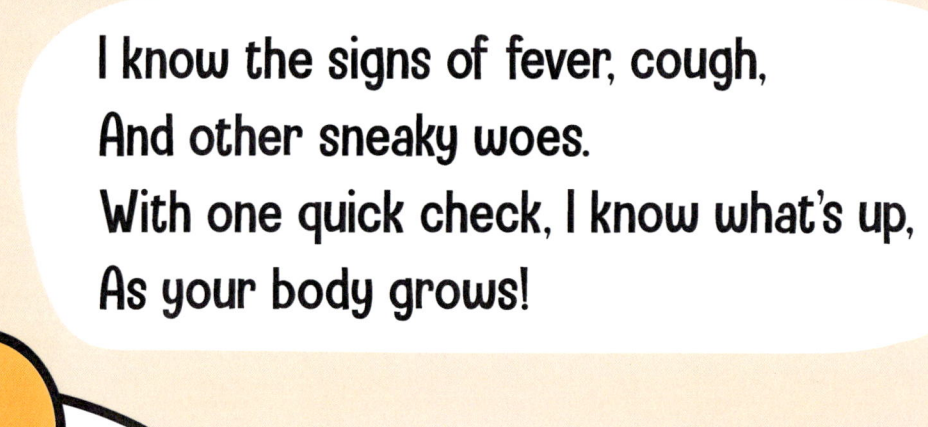

I know the signs of fever, cough,
And other sneaky woes.
With one quick check, I know what's up,
As your body grows!

Check out the fun Doctor Ninja lesson plans at ninjalifehacks.tv

I love to hear from my readers. Email me your feedback or thoughts on what my next story should be at info@ninjalifehacks.tv   Yours truly, Mary

 @marynhin   @GrowGrit
#NinjaLifeHacks

 Ninja Life Hacks

 Mary Nhin   Ninja Life Hacks

 @officialninjalifehacks

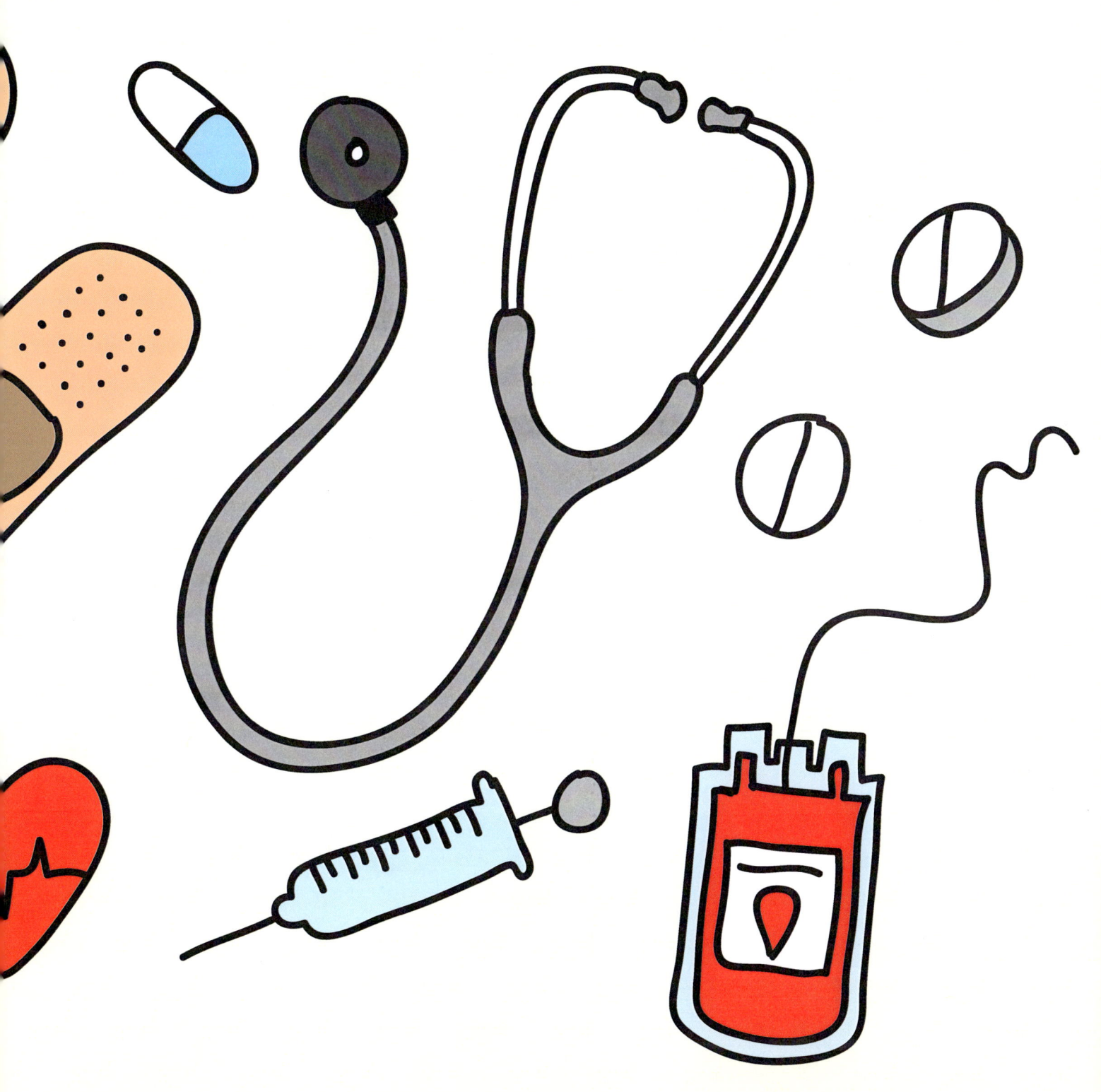

www.ingramcontent.com/pod-product-compliance
Lightning Source LLC
Chambersburg PA
CBRC091453160426
43209CB00024B/1887